OUMAR HILL

PASSION WITHIN

BIRTH OF THE PASSIONPRENEURS

WORKBOOK

> FIND SOMETHING YOU'RE PASSIONATE ABOUT AND KEEP TREMENDOUSLY INTERESTED IN IT.
>
> [JULIA CHILD]

Discover Your Passion Today

Copyright © 2014 | Oumar Hill

Printed in the United States of America

All rights reserved.

"I love to travel down the road that has not been created yet. Take a leap of faith and go down the path not visible."

#Passionpreneurs

Foreword

Discover Your Passion Today was created from *The Passion With-In*, produced by the author of this workbook. It was created to give the readers a chance to mentally go where the author ventured when he was trying to define his passion. Often asking him self what, when and how, but rarely coming up with an answer until he searched deeper within. Now the author has taken the time to share his thoughts and trials with the reader to help the reader discover their internal passions and dreams. This workbook will be helpful if you're going through adversity, a life-changing event, a setback or anything, which requires deep thought. There have been multiple moments in the author's life where he wanted to quit, but he couldn't. He found away to muster up the courage and passion to move forward and you will too after you finish reading this workbook. Once we make a conscious decision to move forward, our strength, decision-making capabilities and confidence will be increased. Some of the hardest questions the author faced on his journey were the following: What do I want to become? What happens if my significant others dies? How do I move forward if I lose my job? I love my job, but it does not make enough money for me; what should I do? When these questions surfaced in the author's life, he felt limited to the lack of funding and opportunity around him. But with prayer, things began to turn around for him and work out for the better, so now he is sharing his steps with you to get through and succeed.

This workbook will share some of the techniques I used to help me discover my passion and how it led to my purpose of writing and teaching others how to become passionpreneurs. What is a passionpreneur? Passionpreneurs place following their dreams as one of their top three priorities in life. This workbook will help you think like a passionpreneur, and you will eventually become one as you journey towards following your dreams and making them come true.

Why is this book for you?
Let me count the ways.......

1. If you ever felt like dreaming.
2. If you are starting over.
3. If you are lost and just need to find your way.
4. If you want to find something new about yourself or awaken something internally special to you.
5. If you are focused on finding a solution instead of discussing the problem.
6. If you are not satisfied with settling.
7. If you never quit on yourself.
8. If you believe in your self-confidence and self-worth

If any of the statements above apply to you, then this book is for you!

Passionpreneurs are those who seek out happiness instead of wealth, still in search of freedom and opportunity but for a greater good, business ventures that not only satisfy a financial need but also help them reach self-actualization. These individuals are led by fulfillment and not by financial gain, even though financial wellness will overflow with passion.

Expectations:

1. Expect to think outside the box.
2. Strengthen your weaknesses.

3. Smile as you discover your purpose.
4. Discover your passionpreneur traits.
5. Change your perspective of thinking.

Principles for Becoming a Passionpreneur
- Push the expectations and raise the bar to the next level.
- Take a negative and turn it into a positive.
- Realize that quitting is not an option.
- Be bold and work with conviction.
- Focus on providing a solution and moving forward in a positive direction.

Reader Responsibilities:
1. Bring content to the discussion.
2. Be prepared to work.
3. Don't give up on yourself.
4. Everything will not be an easy fix, but work through it.
5. Stay positive and don't complain.

Goals of the Workbook:
1. Assist the reader in finding their passion.
2. Help the reader follow their dreams.
3. Provide real life exercises to stimulate thought and track progress.
4. Provide a template for mental development.

Takeaways:
1. Confidence and self-assurance.
2. Workbook with key internal information from the reader(s).
3. A new perspective.
4. Knowledge that God can fix anything.

~PUBLIC SERVICE ANNOUNCEMENT~
This book is not a magic wand and cannot make you an instant millionaire after reading it. This book will give the readers the opportunity to change their lives, thoughts and actions, which may lead to happiness, success, prosperity and overcoming adversity.

Table of Contents

INTRODUCTION 8
    Structure 8
    What can you find inside? 8
    How to get the most from your reading 8
    Who can benefit from this book? 10
    Symbols 10
    Author's Message 11

LESSON 1: BUILD A STRONG FOUNDATION 13
    Focus 13
    Faith 15
    Fundamentals 16

LESSON 2: DEFINE SOURCES OF HAPPINESS 19
    Passion Fruit 22
    Passion Angels 22

LESSON 3: DEFINE YOU 25
    Think like you have a month to live 25

LESSON 4: ACTION PLAN 31
    Create a passion plan 31

LESSON 5: FIND THE PASSION WITHIN 35
    Believe in your ability 35
    Understand your worth 36
    Find the spark within you 36
    Listen to your instinct 38

LESSON 6: MANAGE LIFE 41
    Principles of Success 41
    Principles for managing life 44

LESSON 7: WORK SMARTER 47
- Turn your fear into strength 47
- Associate with great people 49
- Be original 51

LESSON 8: PASSION PYRAMID 53
- Level 1—Idea 54
- Level 2—Passion 54
- Level 3—Hard work 54
- Level 4—Purpose 55
- Level 5—Success 55
- Level 6—Happiness 56
- Level 7—Give back 56

LESSON 9: BENEFITS 59
- Benefits of following your passion 59
- Silver lining benefits 61

LESSON 10: PASSION LIFE CYCLE 63
- Defining your passion zone 64
- Perfecting your passion 64

PASSION JOURNEY JOURNAL 68

Introduction

Oumar Javaun Hill presents to you this book, *Discover Your Passion Today Workbook*! This workbook contains the author's thoughts, questions, and answers the author manifested during to those questions he discovered during his journey to find his passion. This will be the first of three workbooks that will help you develop a holistic approach for loving yourself and following your dreams. The other workbooks are *Loving Yourself Part 1* and *Loving Yourself Part 2*.

Purpose

The purpose of this workbook is to further emphasize the topics discussed in *The Passion Within* Book and give the readers the opportunity to fully engage in discussion with themselves and others to make their dreams more realistic. This workbook contains the author's thoughts, questions, and answers the author manifested during his journey to find his passion for helping others. The information enclosed will be fruitful for the readers and help them fully provoke their deepest thoughts and take the first steps to making their dreams come true.

Structure

The workbook is broken down into five sections, each section focusing on a different area of development to generate a holistic view of passion, which will lead to purpose. Each chapter will start with an explanation of the chapter and a real world comparison and then the readers will be asked a series of questions and/or exercises to complete. At the end of each chapter, the reader will be able to maintain a diary of weakness and strengths to help monitor the things they need to improve. At the end of the workbook, readers will have the ability to submit online feedback on the workbook and its effectiveness.

What can you find inside?

The goal of this workbook is to help develop the mindset of a passionpreneur; which is a special person who has made it their business to live a life of passion and purpose, regardless of the social, economic, financial, mental and societal pressures bestowed upon them. This workbook will simplify the thinking process of finding your passion and help keep a record of how to march towards your passion daily. To do this, you must follow your gut feelings and remove yourself from distractions and negative thoughts.

In the *Discover Your Passion, Today* workbook you will be given the chance to reengage the inner childhood memories and dreams you have always wanted to accomplish, as well as develop thorough understanding of your passion and how to maintain it. If desired, readers will have the opportunity to record and use the information in a group setting to share their ideas with their peers or coworkers. The intent of this workbook is to develop the reader's positive perspective with regards to passion and remain focused.

Passionpreneurs sacrifice, plan and focus on the end goal of living life to the fullest with passion. Do not walk away from dreams; they are not too big to accomplish. We just have to come up with a strategy on how to follow our dreams and how to sustain our current way of living. The easy way out is not an option; the choice of quitting does not live in our house (mind). Enjoy the journey of finding yourself and your passion.

How to get the most from your reading

To get the maximum food for thought from this book, readers will be expected to spend a minimum of 30 minutes to read one section per day and complete the related exercises. Once the exercises are completed, you are expected to record your mental findings, stimulations and passion points to help you reach the next level in your life. Taking the time to read or reread the information carefully will allow you the opportunity to fully understand the lesson, your thoughts and ways to improve. Changing our circumstances takes consistency and patience, so don't rush anything.

Readers are expected to spend a defined amount of time to read and study your passion without any disruption or distraction. This means reading without a cell phone and television. You will be required to dedicate yourself to your thoughts and dreams to become a passionpreneur. The success of this workbook is not determined by the content it provides, rather the determining factor will be yourself and the commitment you provide through your input and self-discipline. It would be wise to set aside a portion of your study time to journal your thoughts and connect them to your actions, as well as create a record of goals and objectives. Instead of memorizing your thoughts, write them down and revisit them every day until they become muscle memory in your brain, a part of you. Using flashcards is a viable way to study your passion. You will have to determine what works best for you.

After completing each section, go back to the front of each chapter and review the goals of the chapter to verify you accomplish each goal. Place a check mark under each goal you accomplished and proceed to the next section. If you do not complete all of the objectives goal, reread the section with a group or partner and get their point of view. Let them determine if you have reached the goal or not. Oftentimes we cannot tell for ourselves. These exercises are designed to be completed on an individual and/or group basis so that the information could be validated by your peers.

Who can benefit from this book?

This workbook is dedicated to anyone who is looking to change their life, business and relationship for the better with passion and purpose. Although this workbook focuses on passion, it will also discuss faith, fighting fear, purpose, leadership and team building. Specific individuals who may learn the most from the information inside include:

- Dreamers
- Entrepreneurs
- Out-of-the-box thinkers
- Passionate People

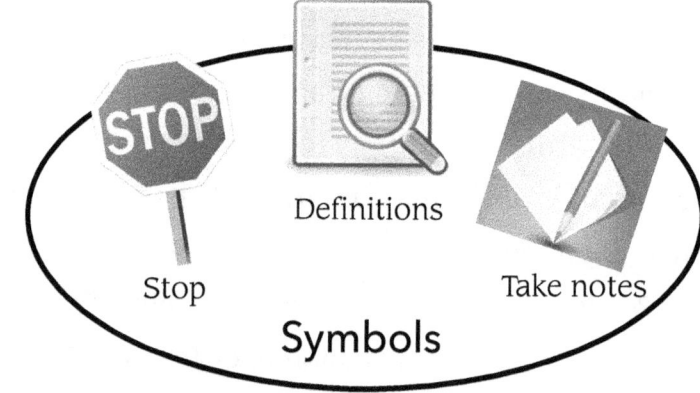

Author's Message

Thank you for taking the time to read this workbook. I have met people from all over the world who are afraid or just in a situation where they don't have the opportunity to follow their dreams, but you do. This is a blessing, so don't take your dreams lightly. Please enjoy the exercises and remember, once you awake your passion, you are responsible for making sure your dreams come true through positive thoughts, continuous repetition of positive actions and believing in yourself. We all go through bad times and adversity, but ultimately, we determine how we react after these situations. I would not be where I am today if I had not failed, fallen down or been rejected. Through all of these things, God makes our dreams possible, so take the time to enjoy your growth and maturation. Its okay and everything will be alright.

Be Prepared to:
1. To think out loud.
2. Strengthen your faith in self.
3. Love your journey.
4. Dig deep inside of you.
5. Change your mindset.
6. Grow and Mature.
7. Read with purpose.

When the author refers to *passion*, he is referring to the fulfillment and contentment we get from doing the things we love with the people we love, true and unconditional passion and purpose.

~GOD IS GOOD~

Passion Agreement Requirements

To complete your introduction to the realm of passionpreneurship, you have to sign your life away. You are requested to dedicate yourself to your wildest dreams and desires and to give your best effort. If any of the items listed below is not something you are currently doing, by signing this document, you agree to work towards changing your life to satisfy the requirements. By signing this agreement, you agree to dedicate yourself to your passion!

As an innovator of my destiny, I will dedicate myself to the following:

- Acknowledge that God is good through all things.
- Speak positively at all times (minimum 80% of the time).
- Spend 30 minutes per day reading my workbook.
- Create a journal of my findings for each section.
- Develop a personal quiet place or sanctuary.
- If in a group setting, I will add to the group discussion.
- Share my story with others.
- Be faithful to my passion and purpose in life.
- Think with purpose throughout each exercise.
- Be accountable for my own actions and studying.
- Help someone else find his or her passion.
- Complete one good deed per day.

_____

(Sign here)

Lesson 1: Build a Strong Foundation
PASSION

Before you begin to step towards your destiny, you need to find out how strong your faith, focus and fundamental life skills (Big Three) are to reach the next level. Everything in life has levels, so we have to know who we are before we can determine where we are going. I believe our steps have been predetermined by a higher power, the choices and actions are left to us to master. The stronger the foundation, the longer the house will stand and withstand the storms ahead. **Translation:** when we build a foundation of positive things in our lives, circle of friends and thoughts, we begin to believe in the possible and defy the impossible.

Life can be a bit difficult and unpredictable. So to build our dreams, we need to strengthen our Big Three.

Levels of Our Foundation
1. **Focus**—I will not let anything distract me from my path.
2. **Faith**—I will believe in my dreams when others count me out.
3. **Fundamentals**—I will live with a fundamental understanding of what I want versus what I need and what skills I need to achieve my passion.

One of the most important pieces of finding our passion is to have the faith to hang in there and see things through along with the courage to believe in our ability. Having faith in a greater good has carried me from the pits to the clouds in the blink of an eye. I could have just quit and given up on life, there was something instilled in me by my parents and siblings that sticks to my soul which allows me to continue to believe when there is no reason to believe. My faith has never led me in the wrong direction and has always helped me feel encouraged and stimulated.

1. Our faith will be tested throughout the process of pursuing our passion.
2. Faith will give us the strength to believe in things we cannot see.
3. Faith will help you complete the impossible.

If it's meant to be, it shall be, and desire will reveal itself through our intentions. The funny thing about passion is it seeps through our pores without explanation, and it is often questioned: *"How did he do that?"* People can recognize passion and purpose in others from miles away. The goal is learning how to discover the passion within you.

PRINCIPLES OF A STRONG FOUNDATION
1. Stay FOCUSED.
2. Keep the FAITH.
3. Work on your FUNDAMENTALS.

Focus

Check the box next to the items that distract you while attempting to focus:

- ☐ Television
- ☐ Internet/Social Media
- ☐ Negative Friends
- ☐ Positive Friends
- ☐ Meditation
- ☐ Cell Phone
- ☐ Job

- ☐ Past Relationship
- ☐ Fear of Failure
- ☐ School
- ☐ Bullies
- ☐ Money
- ☐ Family
- ☐ Other_____

What is Passion?
Passion (noun): a strong feeling of enthusiasm or excitement for something or about doing something: a strong feeling (such as anger) that causes you to act in a dangerous way: a strong sexual or romantic feeling for someone.

Record all the items that prevent you from focusing. Now commit to dedicating one hour per day focusing on your dreams, eliminating distractions and concentrating on building a stronger mental foundation. You have to build the faith in the beginning so you can withstand the pitfalls and the hatred you will encounter while on your journey to live a happy and passionate lifestyle. Happiness comes with a price. Be prepared with faith, focus and fundamentals to stay on course and finish what you start.

Faith

"Faith comes from hearing the message, and the message is heard through the word of Christ."
(Rom. 10:17)

Check the boxes beside the statements that are true:
- ☐ 1. Faith is not going to help me reach my dreams.
- ☐ 2. Faith will not make me a millionaire.
- ☐ 3. Fundamentals are the key to success. Success is doing the right thing over and over again until I become great.
- ☐ 4. Fundamental skills are not important to learn.
- ☐ 5. All things are possible through focus and faith.
- ☐ 6. Winners focus during tough times and lean on their faith in their ability.

If you picked 3, 5 and 6, you are absolutely correct about what it takes to build a strong foundation to following and living a life of fun, happiness and favor.

The power of a person lies within the three F's and determines the good from the great.

What is Purpose?
Purpose (noun): the reason for which something is done or created or for which something exists. God has given us a purpose to live. Purpose is life and passion is the fuel that feeds life.

Fundamentals

Living with and walking with a purpose says a lot about a person. In order to do this we need to have an understanding of our wants versus our needs and have the ability to differentiate between the two, even when we don't want to. This is called self-discipline and it is critical to assuring the pursuit of your dreams and making sure they remain a priority in your life. It is not what you do in the light that will determine your success, it is what you do when no one is looking that will determine your destiny. DO THE RIGHT THING!

We all have wants and this is not a bad thing. It's often an indicator of who we really are and what we desire from our thoughts. It also defines the level of work we have done or the lack thereof.

Examples:
I want to be young; I also need to be thankful for the age I reached.
I want a Bentley; I also need to focus on getting from point A to B.
I want to eat ice cream all day; I also need a healthy diet to maintain my health.

Now it's your turn.
Example:
I want___LOVE___; I also need___RESPECT, INTEGRITY__& HONESTY.

I want_____; I also need_____.
I want_____; I also need_____.
I want_____; I also need_____.

The common problems we all face today are our health and financial stability, both of which need to be balanced by managing our wants versus our needs. If we are trying to lose weight we can't eat what they want, we have to only eat what we need. It is the management of our wants that helps us obtain our bigger needs in life. However, if they consume the proper portions of food covering their needs the weight will fall off quicker. The same goes for a person seeking financial stability. To reach financial wellness we have to focus on our needs and less of our wants. I tell people all the time, do not focus on how much money you make, rather focus on how much you save and pay yourself first. The key to determining wants versus needs, is to understand the bigger picture and ultimate purpose of your journey.

Once we realize our needs versus our wants, we can evaluate the skills we have versus those we don't have. This sets the baseline high and gives us a barometer to gauge our progress. Once we capture the skills we have, we will simultaneously understand the skills we are lacking.

Step one, list the skills you have NOW.

1. _____ 6. _____
2. _____ 7. _____
3. _____ 8. _____
4. _____ 9. _____
5. _____ 10. _____

Step two, list the skills you do NOT have.

1. _____ 6. _____
2. _____ 7. _____
3. _____ 8. _____
4. _____ 9. _____
5. _____ 10. _____

 **Step three, list the skills of the top people who have your "dream job."**

1. _____   6. _____
2. _____   7. _____
3. _____   8. _____
4. _____   9. _____
5. _____ 10. _____

Compare the data gathered from steps 1 and 3, and cross out the similar skills. Next, record the remaining skills and make a list of skills you need to acquire. Work on building the skills you don't have and enhancing the skills you do have every day. This will be a fundamental foundation of skills, confidence and self-assurance that you can use to compete for your dream job. A plan of action is not effective unless you take the action upon yourself to be great.

Lesson 2: Define Sources of Happiness
PURPOSE

Happiness is what we all strive for in life, to share our destiny with our parents, friends and children. To smile and laugh together and uplift each other in times of difficulty, understanding the brevity of life and the delicacy of moments shared with our loved ones. The powerful thing about following our passion is it gives the individual the utmost fulfillment and happiness because they are doing something they actually love doing. We need to define the things in our life that bring us the most joy. Happiness, which is the opposite of stress and drama, makes us feel warm inside and releases the burden we carry on our shoulders every day.

For me, there are four sources of happiness:

God—Faith, favor, and purpose.

Family—Relatives, friends and associates.

Life—Career, passion, and leisure activity.

Choices—Maturation, integrity, gratitude and learning from mistakes.

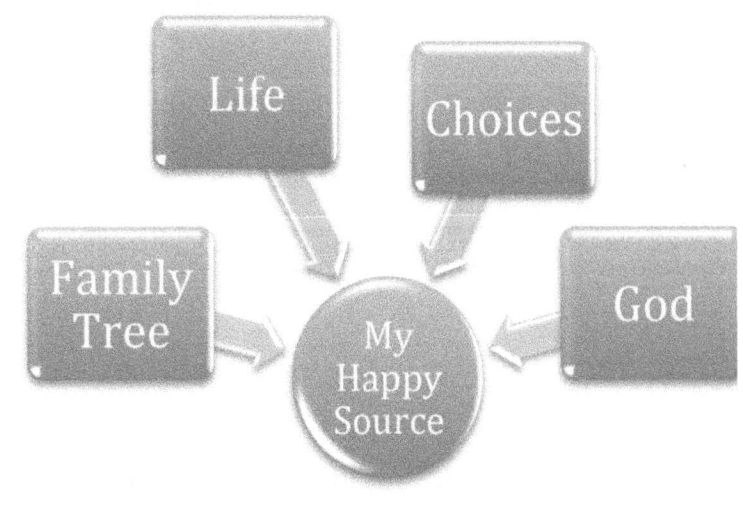

These sources of happiness helped me get through bad days and appreciate the good days. We never know when we will need these sources the most but the first two sources: God and family will always be there when you need them. Life and the choices we make are like the stock market and they tend to go up and down but if we work at both, things will begin to work in our favor.

Define your smiling moments.

These are the moments that give you the most joy and excitement. For example, being able to wake up to the breath taking smile of my daughter brings me joy and being able to spread positivity through my writings. Now it's time to capture your smiling moments:

_____
_____
_____
_____
_____
_____
_____
_____
_____

Rank the Happy Sources from your perspective.

Rank them by what brings you the most fulfillment, joy and satisfaction.

1. _____   A. Family
2. _____   B. Life
3. _____   C. Choices
4. _____   D. GOD

It's okay if you have other things that bring you joy. List them on the next page. The goal is to recognize positivity in all the things that help us smile.

1. _____
2. _____
3. _____
4. _____
5. _____
6. _____

PRINCIPLES TO BECOMING HAPPY

1. Love your family.
2. Love your GOD.
3. Make better choices.
4. Love the cards dealt by life.
5. Don't focus on complaining.
6. Stay humble.

When you get mad, you do the following: _____.
If a person does something to you, are you focused on getting them back, or on forgiving them? Your happiness is dependent on your reactions to people and those you choose to associate with. From the list above, you will begin to develop your list of passion angels and fruit. Passion angels and fruits are people which propel us closer to our purpose in life, on purpose or accidentally. Passion angels will keep you going in the right direction and keep your eye on the goal. Passion fruit provides knowledge, resources and the tools to satisfy your walk towards your purpose. These are the people you will most likely never forget and who will have had the biggest impact on your life. Passion angels are equivalent to a navigation system in a vehicle; they lead you in the right direction, avoid road blocks, and let you know if you have strayed off the path.

Passion Fruit

My mother is a passion angel who dropped passion fruit every day of my life: "Go to school," "Do your best," "Never give up" and "God is good." The road to living with passion is a long road filled with bumps, we should surround ourselves with positive and passionate friends who continuously inject positive vibes and affirmation, we can get through anything. Passion is meant to be spread and not depressed; if we encounter a negative spirit, we should remove ourselves from the equation. Negativity is contagious. We are whom we associate with daily.

Passion Angels

Passion angels are the navigation system in the car. When the car is in drive, it uses fuel to move forward but needs the navigation system to direct us to our destination. Without navigation, we would be stuck with following the directions of strangers or reading a piece of paper while driving. If we don't have passion angels to push, motivate, and teach us along the way, we may sway off our path. This group, passion angels, reduces the time it takes to find success, passion and love. Having passion angels in our corner is a blessing and it makes our journey worth it.

My first passion angel was my late aunt, Gertrude. Her courage, spirit, stature and values have stayed with me throughout my life. I was graced with her presence for only 14 years and they were the best years of my life, full of passion fruit. Taken away too soon by cancer, her soul lives within me; she has instilled passion within me as a young man. She was mentally strong, educated, career driven, gave the worst spankings, and could burn in the kitchen.

List the names of the passion angels in your life and thank them.

Life is short and we need to always appreciate the people who have had a profound effect on our life, for without them, we would not have the opportunities we have today. Now list the top passion fruit moments in your life.

1. _____
2. _____
3. _____
4. _____
5. _____
6. _____
7. _____

> **Looking for opportunities to share your testimony with others will often lead you to your destiny and purpose.**

List the Passion Fruit moments (moments you learned a life lesson)

1. _____
2. _____
3. _____
4. _____
5. _____
6. _____
7. _____

Lesson 3: Define You
FAITH

You have to define what you really want in life to discover your passion. People can assume and speculate your desire to do something, but only you know the true extent of your desires and intentions. Steps have to be taken in the direction of your dreams. You have to define who you are, what makes you happy, your thoughts and beliefs. Steps have to be taken in the direction of your dreams. Define who you are with regard to what makes you happy, your thoughts and your beliefs.

I recall sending an email out to my dearest friends asking for their advice on a book title and one friend said, "You don't know how to write, who is writing this book for you?" I was angry at first, but I realized he was not with me through the writing classes, documentation for various government agencies or writing for doctors' publications on clinical trials. He did not know the desire that was within me, he only knew of my athletic ability. We cannot wait for others to define who we are; we have to be proactive in showing the world our gifts and purpose.

The first part is defining the things that make us happy today; the second part is finding the things that made you happy as a child. As adults, we are bombarded with responsibility, policies and procedures. Too often we defer from chasing our dreams because our reality is paying bills and putting food on the table. This way of living and thinking has to stop. You can be happy and earn a substantial income doing the things you love.

What have you always dreamed of doing?

_____
_____
_____
_____
_____
_____
_____

What is holding you back from going after your dream(s)?

_____
_____
_____
_____
_____
_____
_____

As you visualize your dreams, record the reasons why they have not materialized; this section will provide you with extra energy to begin writing a plan to turn your dreams into your reality. The things holding you back are often the things that, once mastered, will lift us greatness. Do not fear what do not have, just perfect your talents and work hard every day. When defining yourself, focus on your skills and no one else's. Think as if you were going to die tomorrow, and today was your last day on earth. What would you do differently? Now do not quit your job just yet; begin to think as if it could happen because you don't know when your day will come.

Think like you have a month to live

Imagine your doctor called and said, "Good morning, you have a month to live." What would you do? What would you think? What would be your priorities? These moments should be how we attack every day and the challenges we face in life. We need to wake up thinking our last days are unknown and we have a month to create a legacy for our family and friends.

List your thoughts if you knew you were going to die in 1 month. Answer the following three questions.

1. How would you approach your life differently, knowing what you know now?

   _____
   _____
   _____
   _____

2. How would you treat others?

   _____
   _____
   _____
   _____
   _____

3. How would you spend your time?

   _____
   _____
   _____
   _____
   _____

To find and obtain our passion, we need complete focus and commitment to sustain our energy and faith in the process. Dreams are meant to be fulfilled. If you are having a problem answering the questions, its okay, life changing events are not easy and require deep thought to make the right decisions. To help you devise a plan of action, I have listed some additional life changing questions for you to ponder.

1. If you could change one thing in the world, what would it be?

    _____
    _____
    _____

2. If you could live anywhere in the world, where would it be?

    _____
    _____
    _____

3. If you could be a famous person for one day, whom would it be?

    _____
    _____
    _____

4. If you had one wish, what would it be?

    _____
    _____
    _____

5. If asked to speak at a college graduation, what would you say?

    _____
    _____

6. What three things are most important to you now that you have 1 month to live?

_____

_____

_____

7. You can only see 3 people for the rest of your life. Who are they?

_____

_____

_____

These questions force us to be open, honest and direct with ourselves and way of thinking. When death is introduced into the picture of life, we tend to make decisions faster because time is of the essence, and we tend to focus on the silver linings of life. We have to get to a place or comfort zone where we are doing the things we enjoy most and around the people we love most. This is the only way we can live a fulfilling life. Finish this section by answering the question we were all asked as kids: "What do you want to be when you grow up?" Think deeply about the things that move you the most. The goal is to try to regain the happiness you had as a child and adolescent. Following your passion and dreams is a very bold and courageous act that will require discipline, commitment and energy to complete.

PRINCIPLES OF DEFINING YOU
1. Be honest with yourself.
2. Dive deep into your thoughts.
3. Think of what makes you happy.
4. Think with purpose.

Lesson 4: Action Plan
FAMILY

Now that you have built a foundation, know what makes you happy, defined your wants and self-identity, now you can begin to develop a plan to move towards your passion with purpose. Think of yourself as a business and reorganize your way of thinking to refocus on the bigger picture. The first task is to develop a goal with objectives and actions to move you closer to your goal. Think of it in three levels. The highest level is the actual goal. The middle level is the objectives we need to execute to accomplish these goals. The lowest level is compromised of small steps in each objective to being and complete.

After setting your goals and objectives, begin to map out your plan to find passion, simultaneously building self-esteem and confidence. When developing this plan for your goals, make sure they are SMART goals. SMART goals are:

1. **Specific**—what would you like to do?
2. **Measurable**—Track your progress -How much or how many?
3. **Achievable**—be realistic.
4. **Relevant**—how important is it to you?
5. **Time-based**—what is your expected date of completion?

Your goals help to define your priorities in life.

Goal writing example: My goal is to develop an increased understanding of my passion by the end of the year.

TAKING CONTROL OF MY LIFE!

Take a shot at writing down your SMART goal for following your passion
TAKE YOUR TIME & THINK! DON'T RUSH!

_____
_____
_____

Objectives writing example:
- I will interview three people who are already successful in the field I want to join.
- I will find three books related to my dreams and read them within 6 months.
- I will identify three non-profits that are involved in the community and partner with them within 9 months.

Take a shot at writing objectives that map back to the overall goal.
TAKE YOUR TIME & THINK! DON'T RUSH!

1. Objective

   _____
   _____

2. Objective

   _____
   _____

3. Objective

   _____
   _____

4. Objective

   _____
   _____

5. Objective

_____

_____

Once you have your goals and objectives connected, create a transition plan or list the actions needed to work towards your objectives. When writing your action steps, remember to be honest with yourself. The worst thing you could do is lie to yourself. To follow passion, you have to love yourself and be selfish enough to put your dreams in high priority. The more open and honest you are will determine the feasibility of your plan for making your dreams come true.

Passion is a hard thing to do sometimes; but when it's real, we will sacrifice everything without hesitation. Passion is the feeling we have inside which makes us feel good, loved, and self-worthy. It helps us go to sleep, wake up, and get our days started.

Check True or False

T_____ F_____ Goals are critical for success and objectives are measurable.

T_____ F_____ Goals are not important to important people.

T_____ F_____ Goals must map into our objectives.

T_____ F_____ Actions step come before writing your objectives.

T_____ F_____ Great leaders maintain a level of honesty with themselves and their team.

Create a passion plan.

Now that you have an idea of what your passion is, it's time to create a plan. But before you do anything, you will need to gather all the information you have thus far (goals, objectives, poster and vision board). I have achieved my success in life because I always had a plan and I was very flexible in updating my plan with new ideas and concepts.

Map out the top seven steps to reach your objectives and work on each step one day of the week for at least one hour. If you have more than seven steps, you can double up the actions on a certain day, one in the morning and another in the evening. Just make sure you dedicate one hour to following your dream with purpose. Record your results. Repeat this task every Sunday until each of your objectives is complete.

Weekly Action Steps Planner

1. _____

2. _____

3. _____

4. _____

5. _____

6. _____

7. _____

Purpose101 - Your purpose is an overarching goal for you to accomplish in your lifetime. It provides direction for every day we live.

Lesson 5: Find the Passion Within
SELF-LOVE

Find something deep within yourself to assist you with pursuing your dreams and turning it into reality. As you grow and mature during your journey, you will realize what is of great importance to your life. Focusing your attention on our passion, then having the courage to pursue it is a blessing in itself. Life is meant to be enjoyed, shared and improved every day we are alive. Everything we have ever needed is within us and waiting to be discovered. Passion is one dream, step, or change away. The formula is to find happiness, define yourself and then find your passion. Most importantly you must believe in yourself and your abilities.

Believe in your ability. Do you believe you can achieve? If you don't, who will? It will take an encouraging person to encourage others. I have never met a great leader who did not believe in his/her abilities. Before we lead others with passion, we have to define and determine who we are.

a. Do you believe you can accomplish something that has never been accomplished by anyone in your family or circle of friends?
   _____

b. Can you change your generational curse?
   _____

c. How many hours a day do you dedicate to social media versus your craft?_____

Understand your worth.

You are more than enough and are more than capable of doing anything with discipline and persistence. What is driving you to desire more out of life? If money lost value, what profession would you do for free? This is where you need to start looking for hints leading you to your passion. Answer the following questions:

a. If money did not have value, what would you do for a living?

_____

b. What makes you smile out of control?

_____

Find the spark within you.

This may be the need to increase knowledge and wisdom, or just the need to improve your current circumstances. Whatever the case may be, something inside of you drives you, and you have to find this. Once you find your "it factor" that sparked your passion, you will need to expand on the feeling or motivation. Ride the wave of motivation until you reach the shore, and then begin to look for the next wave to carry you out to sea and do it all over again.

Develop a mental vision board in your mind, capturing everything that inspires and motivates you to want more. Then break your vision into three sections titled: "The things I love to do," "The things I want to do," and "The things I just do." The goal is to do more things we love and want to do.

Answer these questions.

a. What drives you to want more?

_____

b. How important is it to you to see your dreams come true (Rank 1-10, 10 the highest)? ____

c. If you could pass on one attribute to your children, what would it be?

_____

d. If you had a vision board, what pictures would you have on the vision board?

_____

e. What is your legacy and how do you want to be remembered? What do you want your family and friends to remember most about you?

_____

_____

I want to leave my daughter a legacy to follow and to pass the lessons I learned from my parents to her. I do not just want to be known as the guy with a nice car or big bank account. I would rather be remembered for my warm smile and words of encouragement. When we do things with passion and purpose, we are building a legacy for all to follow and replicate.

What do you want to be remembered for?
- ☐ Nice Person
- ☐ Smart
- ☐ Rich
- ☐ Leadership
- ☐ Material Things
- ☐ Careers
- ☐ Relationship
- ☐ Failures
- ☐ Education
- ☐ Family
- ☐ Other_____

Listen to your instinct.

This is one of the most powerful rules to follow when you look deep within yourself to find what drives you. Learning to listen to your instincts is critical to the success or failure of your dreams. To me, intuition is having the mental foresight to know something without being able to explain how we came to that conclusion rationally. This is where faith plays a big role in the decision making process. Faith gives us enough time to make it until help arrives. Faith builds strength within and helps us make the right decision.

Passionpreneurs
- Push the expectation and standards bar to the next level.
- Take a negative and turn it into a positive.
- Know that quitting is not an option.
- Focus on providing a solution and moving forward in a positive direction.

Write down your purpose at the beginning of each week.

_____
_____
_____
_____
_____

Task: At the end of the week, write your purpose again without looking at what you have written above. Write it on a separate piece of paper. Eventually, your true purpose will be revealed by the similarities of your thoughts and affirmations.

Lesson 6: Manage Life
INTEGRITY

To effectively manage your life, you have to manage your expectations, fears and how you react to things that are beyond your control. Managing your expectations refers to what success means to you. We all have a different meaning of success, and there is no one right answer, we are all unique with different backgrounds, so when we work in a group setting or build teams, we need to understand what success means to everyone. Once we determine this, we can compromise and create a successful goal for the group. Learning how to manage our fears is essential to obtaining them and most of our fears are developed from our own misconceptions. We scared ourselves out of a blessing. Sometimes we just need to be still and let life take its course. This leads to the next step, which is to stop trying to control things we can't control. Oftentimes when we try to control things beyond our control, they begin to control us.

BE PREPARED TO
1. Manage expectations.
2. Manage fear.
3. Control what you can.
4. Define success.

Principles of Success

Check what success means to you.

- ☐ FAME
- ☐ MONEY
- ☐ HEALTH
- ☐ LOVE
- ☐ WISDOM
- ☐ HELPING OUT
- ☐ SOCIAL LIFE
- ☐ WAKING UP
- ☐ BEING STRONG
- ☐ GETTING UP
- ☐ PROVIDING
- ☐ YOUR KIDS

Task: At the end of the month, record what success means to you, as you grow and mature, the meaning of success may change. The goal is to understand the best things in life are the simple things like family, love, smiling and being happy. Once you record your monthly results, revisit them prior to starting the New Year and create a New Year's resolution based on the data collected from your monthly success findings.

_____
_____
_____
_____
_____

It takes a great deal of training, focus and energy to find your passion and then perfect it. Once you've acquired it, you cannot forget about the future. It is time to look outside of your perspective. This will help you think outside of the box and prevent you from getting in your way. Sometimes we are so submerged in ourselves, we forget to honesty analyze our abilities. It is critical to associate with people who don't mind telling us about our good and bad habits. This tends to reduce fears and build self-esteem. It is my belief that constructive criticism is construction of self, building trust, self-esteem, listening skills and the ability to pay attention to details.

On a separate sheet of paper, write down three things you can't control, pray and then shred the paper.

Each day, practice relinquishing the need to think about things that are out of your control. It is the practice which make us perfect. The ability to learn from our weaknesses, strengths and opportunities will only improve our craft. Remembering there is someone with the same dream, working as hard as we are trying to accomplish it, should be enough internal motivation to push us forward. Although we desperately try to control things; patience, positivity, and prayer works best.

―――――― *TAKING CONTROL OF MY LIFE!* ――――――

Write three things within your control & think about them daily.

_____

_____

_____

Are you investing in yourself, or investing in the drama and stress of others? It is easier to recognize the trouble in others than to recognize our own problems within. If we'd address our own issues, we'd effectively help more people with their problems. This is similar to babysitting someone else's children. We may feel raising children is easy, but not until we have children of our own do we understand the true difficulties and responsibilities of being a parent. It's not easy. The best investment I've made in my life is investing in my dreams. I tell young passionpreneurs all the time, "Put your money where your passion is.

Questions to ask yourself. Circle YES or NO.

1. Do you want the attention or do you want success? YES or NO

2. Are you 100% invested in your dreams? YES or NO
   (If not, you should work towards being 125% invested.)

3. Do you want someone to invest in you? YES or NO
   (If so, you may want to invest in yourself, because people are hesitant to invest their hard-earned money in a person who has not invested in themselves.)

Keeping a circle of positive people around you at all times is very important to thinking positive and looking on the bright side of all situations. On this journey to find your passion find the silver lining, find the positive energy, and learn from the negative.

"Gratitude is the best way to move forward. Be grateful for everything on your journey, keep your head up and heart open; life will not be easy but you are built for the journey. Know that bad days will eventually become good, and make notes

of the positive message you hear each day. The goal is to be a positive water hose spraying positivity all throughout the community to help passion seeds grow. Positive people bring about new ideas and opportunity because they think and live freely without the fear of stress."

Find a checklist below, for you to check off daily, to help you keep in control of yourself and reduce the need to control things outside of you. Every time you exhibit one of the attributes listed below, add a check mark:

- ☐ Humility
- ☐ Gratitude
- ☐ Forgiveness
- ☐ Love
- ☐ Integrity
- ☐ Faith
- ☐ Patience
- ☐ Common Sense
- ☐ Self-Discipline
- ☐ Honesty
- ☐ Intuition
- ☐ Consciousness

> **PRINCIPLES FOR MANAGING LIFE**
> 1. Be prepared for a storm.
> 2. Stay positive and peaceful.
> 3. Define success to you.
> 4. Release stress and drama.
> 5. You are whom you associate with.
> 6. Dreams are hard work.
> 7. Don't give away your power.
> 8. Control yourself.
> 9. Love the journey, good and bad.

Principles for managing life.

Work to be the best person you can every day. You don't have to be perfect, you just have to outwork anyone in your way, which is perfection. Once you work towards perfection, your mistakes will not be as visible and people will begin to think you are perfect. A perfect person's work ethic covers up their mistakes because they realize they are not perfect, they will never let you outwork them. Smile more, because it will take you to the top. Smiling helped me control my emotions and conceal my true feelings of anger and aggression. Following your passion comes with stress, drama, and bad days. But you can face these negative events with positive energy and a smile.

Write down a list of things you are going to work on and try to improve today.

1. _____
2. _____
3. _____
4. _____
5. _____
6. _____
7. _____

Recognize you are blessed! There are people who rarely get the opportunity to have an opportunity, so if you are lucky to have an opportunity, you are blessed and highly favored.

Lesson 7: Work Harder
POSITIVITY

The goal is to work smarter, not harder. This will help us reach our goal and retain our sanity upon arrival. If you are feeling uncomfortable in your current walk of life, career or relationship, it's okay. This means there is room for improvement. The work must start within. The things I feared or was uncomfortable doing gave me the most strength in the long run. For example, talking in front of a crowd or reading books were a nightmare for me as a child, but as an adult, I love reading and talking to people. Just think of your fear as your opportunity.

Fill in the blanks.

The goal for _____ (Date) is to work on my _____. (List weakness) On this day, I will promise to make the most out of my life, career and relationships. I am not afraid of _____ (list weakness) and I will turn it into my strength.

Turn Your Fear into Strength

Fear is meant to be faced and challenged with confidence, boldness and conviction, which will convert your weaknesses to strengths. I understand fear is a part of nature; we can transform this fear into motivation to overcome any obstacle in our life. Once we learn how to live with faith, passion and perseverance, we will reduce our fears enormously. Fear is what we make it and we can reduce it with faith and purposeful thinking. Take the fear test below.

1. To defeat fear you need the following:
    a. God
    b. Faith
    c. Know your weaknesses
    d. Practice, practice
    e. Know your fears
    f. All of the above

PRINCIPLES OF THIS TEST
1. Think with purpose.
2. No wrong answer.
3. Overcome fear.
4. Self- evaluation.

2. What should you do if you become afraid of something?
    a. Stay humble
    b. Make adjustments
    c. Never give up
    d. Talk yourself through positively
    e. Stay focused on your goal
    f. All of the above

3. Do you believe in dreams or nightmares?
    a. Yes
    b. No
    c. Not sure

4. How often do you think about negative versus positive affirmations?
    a. Once a day
    b. Once a week
    c. Once a month
    d. Never

5. What scares you?
   a. Forgetting quickly
   b. Making mistakes
   c. Success
   d. The unknown
   e. Falling down
   f. All of the above

Often times when we fail, we anticipate failure. When traveling towards our passion we do not have time to invest our thoughts and thinking into negativity. We need to perform with 100% of our positive energy and think things through prior to execution. To get over your fears, learn how to control your emotions and thoughts.

Associate with Great People

Sacrifice requires discipline, acceptance, along with hours upon hours of hard work and determination. If the people in your life are not of like mind, then you need to remove yourself and associate with people who uplift you. There is nothing wrong with hanging with people to become better and with purpose. My goal is to make the world a better place, make people wiser, and foster better relationships amongst the diverse ethnicities in the world.

Know when to tell family members and friends, "I love you but you need counseling. Your problems are higher than my pay grade. I am sorry in advance."

Stay away from people who continuously display the following attributes:

- Play the victim
- Over controlling
- Gossiping excessively
- Excess complaining
- Passively listening
- Not focused on a solution
- Narrow minded
- Crying wolf
- Jealousy
- Insecurities

Negative people need attention and will try to prevent you from reaching your goals and happiness. Stay away from passion vampires. These individuals have a negative story every time we encounter them. "My car got towed." "I lost my job." "My rent is overdue." "I'm getting old." The list goes on and on. My motto is "No drama and little stress will keep me blessed."

GIVE THIS LETTER TO NEGATIVE PEOPLE: USE WISELY

Greetings _____ (Negative person's name goes here),

I hope this message finds you in great spirits.

I am blessed and happy to be on a journey of passion, love and happiness. This letter is to inform you of my decision to ignore your negative words and actions because I am so submerged in my happiness and faith, I cannot respond with negative lies or words to rebuke your continuous testimony of negativity. I will positively pray for your well-being even though I know you will say something negative about me to your family, strangers and whomever else will give you an ear to bleed with negativity. The best part about life is living and living with passion because it gives us purpose to be something bigger than ourselves. I WISH YOU POSITIVITY, LOVE AND FAITH IN YOUR LIFE TODAY!

Always remember:
"Let your light shine before men, that they may
see your good deeds and praise your father in heaven." Matt. 5.16
The secret of the battle is won on your knees in prayer.

Love and light to you and stay blessed,
Positive_____ (Your name here) Xoxoxo
P.S. I refuse to be negative

BE ORIGINAL

BE PREPARED TO
1. Lose friends.
2. Gain enemies.
3. Be in fights without knowing.
4. Be hated for no reason.
5. Smile more.
6. Enjoy life.
7. Stand for what you believe.

God has made you perfectly in your own light and form. There has to be some modern ingenuity in creating your passion because it represents your brand and your way of thinking. It is okay to be different; you have the right to be yourself. Being original gives the world a piece of your heart, mind and soul, which cannot be replicated.

Make a list of all things that make you unique.

1. _____
2. _____
3. _____
4. _____
5. _____
6. _____
7. _____
8. _____
9. _____
10. _____

PRINCIPLES OF WORKING SMART
1. Stay away from negative people.
2. Be yourself.
3. Stay Positive.
4. Turn fear into strength.
5. To be great, associate with great.

Once you list those things, do them immediately!

Lesson 8: Passion Pyramid
PERSISTENCE

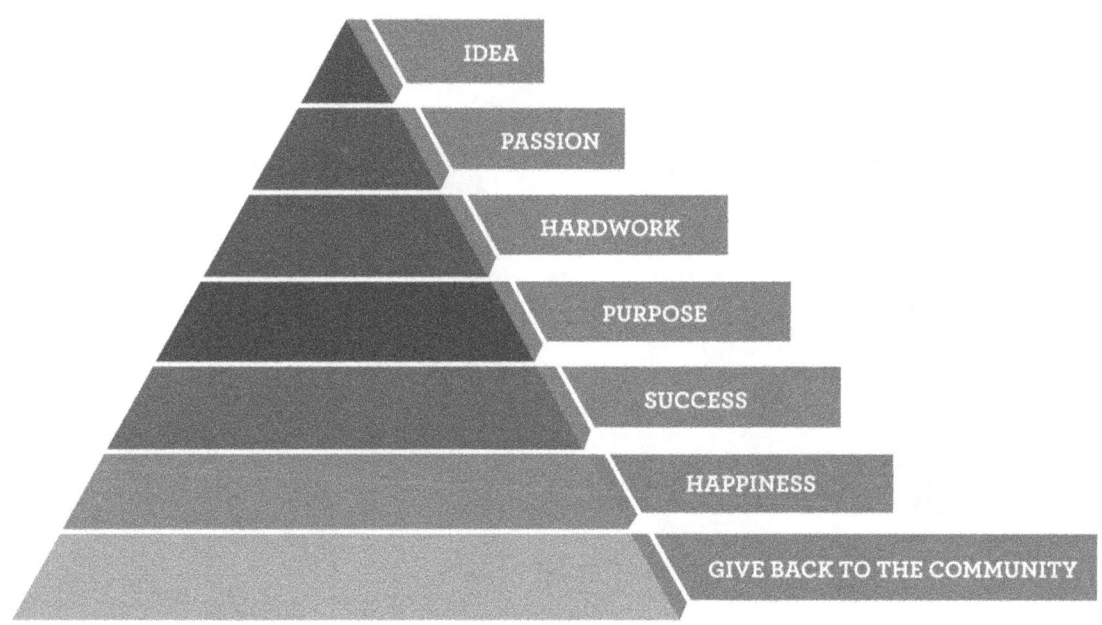

Passion should be in everything we do, from our career to leisure activities, family, relationships and educational endeavors. Passion should be the basis of all our answers to the questions of life. Passion has many levels to it and there are certain things we must do to make sure we make it to the next level. The key to this pyramid is the foundation, which was discussed in the first chapter. I will provide a statement for each phase enclosed regarding the Passion Pyramid, and you will have the opportunity to develop your own passion pyramid in the subsequent writing space.

Level 1—Idea

This is the early stage of creating your dreams and cultivating them into reality. This is where your dreams captivate your mind with the possibility of living the life you want. Happiness will follow.

Now capture your ideas.

_____
_____
_____

Level 2—Passion

Now it is time to expand on the idea of exploring your passion. You have more answers to the questions in the previous level and it is time to walk towards your passion. We have to take the talk from the first level and lead with our actions.

Now capture your ideas.

_____
_____
_____

Level 3—Hard work

Following your passion, you will be challenged, rejected, delayed and doubtful, but with the right attitude and fortitude to keep the faith and keep pushing, you will eventually reach your purpose. The only way this pendulum swings in the positive direction is with a "no quit" attitude, not taking no for an answer, pushing through when others give up, staying the course when the path is not clear, and having a faith in your vision and purpose. When you encounter difficult times, you should have a community of friends, resources and relaxing techniques to help you stay on schedule.

Now capture your ideas.

_____
_____
_____

Level 4—Purpose

My purpose is to share my stories, testimonies and dilemmas from my life to assist others whom may need a helping hand. Purpose includes everything from the concept of a thought to the intangible skills developed along the way to building confidence in your passion and becoming happy in all facets of life. On this level, you should begin to look back on the things you have experienced during your journey and what they meant to you during and after the experience occurred.

Now capture your ideas.

_____
_____
_____

Level 5—Success

Throughout this journey, you have been able to define what success is and what it means to you. Now take the time to relive those things and list the new things in your life which bring you happiness and joy. Success is in the eye of the beholder.

Now capture your ideas.

_____
_____
_____

Level 6—Happiness

It is time to celebrate your journey. You have reached a level that very few people muster up the energy to obtain. You are doing something you love and you are moving closer to fulfilling your purpose. Happiness is addictive and spreads like wild fire. You are happy with the person you are becoming, the things you are doing, and the things you will be doing in the future, and you are happy about the effect you are having on the lives of others.

Now capture your ideas.

_____

_____

_____

Level 7—Give back

Once we find our passion and achieve happiness, it's time to give back and help others achieve the same thing or better. We would not be in the position we are in today if it wasn't for passion angels delivering passion fruit. Now the time has come for you to no longer be the student but the teacher. The ability to give back to the community is a blessing and honor. The best way to spread word of your success is to do something good within the community.

BE PREPARED TO
1. Live with passion.
2. Love without limit.
3. Challenge the status quo.
4. Pay attention to details.

The people within the community are looking for hope and every time they turn around there goes another politician or leader being escorted to jail for some type of illegal activity. When we decide to help others, we actually heal ourselves, and like practicing our craft, we are practicing and making sure we don't fall back into the misery pit of sorrow.

Now capture your ideas.

_____

_____

_____

_____

This was my passion pyramid. If you feel your passion pyramid is different, I have included a blank passion pyramid for you to update and use for your own passion journey.

POINTS OF PASSION PYRAMID

1. Passion is what you make it.
2. Passion is unique.
3. Giving back is the ultimate goal.
4. Passion creates success and happiness.
5. Passion comes with hard work.

Make your passion pyramid. Understand how you think.

1. _____
2. _____
3. _____
4. _____
5. _____
6. _____
7. _____

Lesson 9: Benefits
FULFILLMENT

Benefits of following your passion

There are subliminal benefits to following your passion and oftentimes the effect is easy to spread to others through joy, happiness and excitement. Of course we will have the benefit of being admired by our peers and internal fulfillment, however, there are plenty of other benefits when following your dreams. My passion turns my weakness into strength and gives me the confidence and fortitude that everything will be okay. Here is a list of the benefits I received from following my dream. You can list the benefits you wish to accomplish after reading mine, and once you begin your passion journey, you can revisit your list and make adjustments, if needed.

Benefits I gained from following my passion:

1. **Developed leadership and decision making skills.** Society is full of change, rejection and bad leadership. The individuals who muster the courage, determination and fortitude to lead with passion often sacrifice the most, such as social life, leisure activities and relationships. Leaders spend the majority of their time and energy on activities which bear the most return on passion investment.

2. **Community love.** I took a journey to Ethiopia with my best friend and television show host NuNu Wako, and we traveled through multiple cities there, meeting

people of various ethnicities along the way and spreading love and joy. The ability to travel across the world and share our stories of living in the United States with others is priceless. All of the people there were as curious about us as I was curious about them; these passionate friendships seemed heaven sent. The passion I have for people, humanity and educating others permeated throughout the people I encountered throughout Ethiopia. Sometimes being referred to as Gabe, meaning "lost son" or "God's gift" or "God's son," they thought highly of me and I thought higher of them.

3. **Fueled success.** A person leading with passion will spend the majority of their time thinking and working hard to figure out the next steps. Passion fuels success by giving us the extra fuel to get over the hump, to keep on keeping on. When we think we have created our last inspiration, passion will give us one more idea.

4. **Built confidence.** Passion builds confidence in everything we do. One apple can spoil a bunch, and one good seed can start a garden of positivity. The act of perfecting our craft and getting better every day builds the confidence within us and the people around us.

5. **Taught instinctual perseverance.** Passion does not rely on logic, but more on common sense and a strong faith that what is for you will remain for you. When we are going through hard times, we need to hold on, remain positive and take it one day at a time. Passion will help us heal, see the big picture and overcome obstacles.

6. **Better love life.** Living with passion has a way of making us look loveable. A person that has the determination and self-discipline to follow their dreams no matter what the status quo is saying is pretty powerful and sexy in the eyes of most people. Finding our passion comes with big reward. Not only does loving what we do make us work harder, it also makes us think about the work and makes us smarter.

Silver lining benefits

1. **Positivity all day.** Wake up with a positive mindset and feeling of youthfulness. My message is, "Thank you for waking me up. God, you are good; thank you for the wisdom, favor and the Holy Spirit to make this day better than yesterday."

2. **Ability to heal.** When we go through a negative situation and manage our emotions, we not only come out with discipline, but also with confidence and strength to survive anything with patience.

3. **Forgiveness.** Learn how to forgive others who have wronged you. We never know a person's entire life story. To live, we have to forgive. The burden of bitterness is too heavy to carry.

4. **Manage anger.** When people do things to test our patience, we must dig deep inside of ourselves and maintain our compassion for people who have wronged us. Karma is a good thing only if we have been good to others.

5. **Do not compare yourself to others.** Do not compare the success of others to your own. When we do this, we often compare our failures to others success. This is a mental roadblock from concentrating on our passion, thinking positive and living with purpose. The only person you need to compare yourself to is the person you were yesterday and the day before that.

6. **Being thankful.** Every night before we go to sleep, we should give God thanks for the all the things we enjoyed and endured to create the person we are today. Ask God for understanding and wisdom to help us understand the lessons to be learned.

List the benefits you wish to gain from following your passion.

_____
_____
_____

Lesson 10: Passion Life Cycle
ORIGINALITY

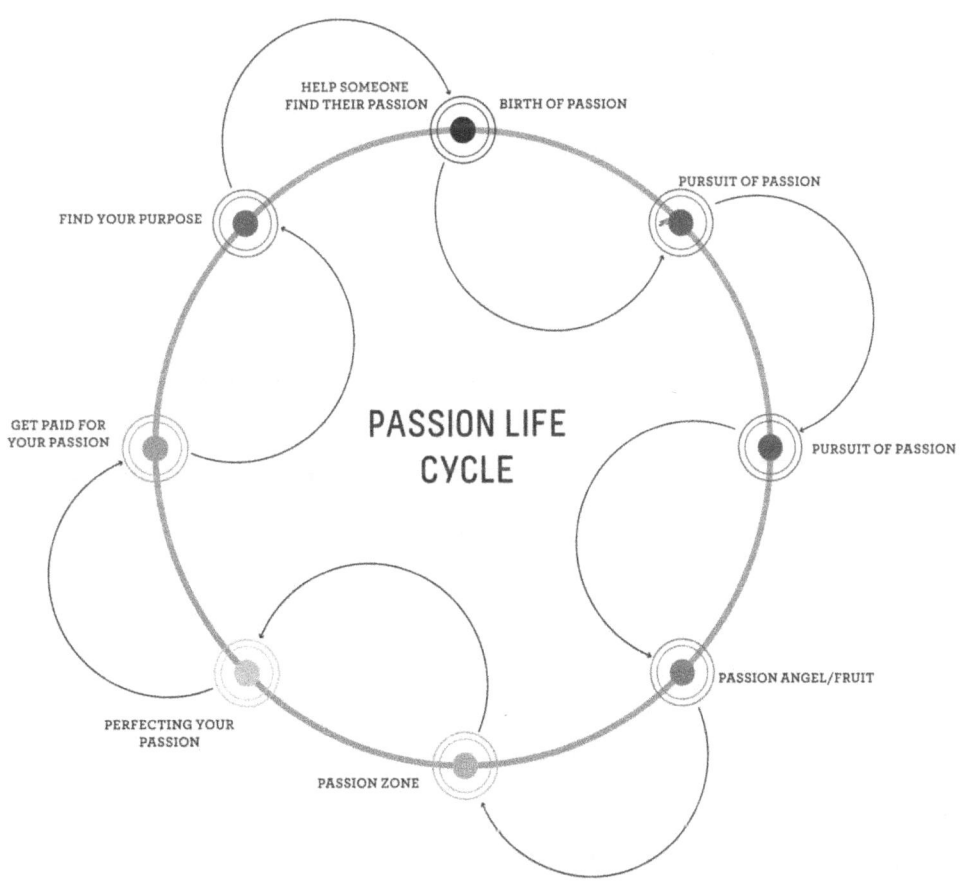

This is the holistic view of creating, chasing and achieving your passion. Similar to the passion pyramid, but takes additional steps to complete the life cycle. We will focus on those steps and how important they are to reaching and keeping our dreams alive.

Defining your passion zone
Define the moment when you are most productive and focused.
_____
_____
_____

Circle the time of day you are most productive.
    1. Morning   2. Evening   3. Night

Perfecting your passion
Once you reach your passion zone and gain confidence, you must perfect your craft. This means it is necessary to keep doing positive things so they become habit forming, but keep it simple. Practice, practice, and practice. My motto is "practice makes perfect and practice is worth it."

To become good at your craft, you need to do the following:
1. Practice
2. Execute on demand
3. Be smart
4. Be confident
5. All the above

To become good at your craft you need to do the following:
1. Follow others
2. Run from your fear
3. Give up on dreams
4. Judge others
5. None of the above

The goal is to find a way to convert your passion into a substantial income to maintain your way of living. Getting paid for your passion is bigger than any financial reward; it involves getting paid with internal joy, happiness, smiling and non-stop laughing. These characteristics will increase our confidence, self-assurance, wisdom, self-esteem and faith. To create a financial reward from your passion, you will need to set up a plan for training yourself, gaining experience and building your brand.

The first step of turning your passion into money is to find a need and fill it with a service. Put the financial reward on the back end and focus on satisfying a need with our skill sets.

1. What need is your passion solving?

_____

_____

_____

_____

Then you need to conduct research, talk to people and focus on filling needs. Search for the pros and cons and develop a plan of action.

2. Who is doing what you want to do and doing it well? Find your competition and how much they get paid.

_____

_____

_____

_____

Invest all of your money in your passion before you invest in other things. Stay focused and always remember, everything that glitters is not gold. Be aware of the sharks in the water and guard your dreams with a passion.

3. Are you investing in yourself first (financially, spiritually, and mentally)?

_____
_____
_____
_____

Create a transition plan. This is a short plan of how you intend to transition your skills into your dream job and how to make the same income without falling behind on bills. Next, sit down and talk to a family member or spouse. Tell them your intentions and get their feedback.

4. Develop a plan after talking with yourself, family and friends.

_____
_____
_____
_____
_____
_____
_____
_____
_____
_____

Things are starting to make sense, especially the bad days. They were preparing us for this moment. Purpose gives us the feeling of fulfillment and being part of something bigger than ourselves. Purpose gives a sense of everlasting happiness, legacy and love for generational happiness. A purposeful life is actually living right and living with a meaning. Purpose is hard to find, but once we find it, we are rarely distracted and deterred. Once we find our passion, our purpose is sure to follow.

5. Define your purpose in life.

_____
_____
_____
_____

TAKING CONTROL OF MY LIFE!

PASSION JOURNEY JOURNAL
~DAY 1~

In this journal, capture your thoughts in the morning, midday and right before you go to bed. The key is to dedicate more time to investing in you mentally every day. Print the pages and copy to extend beyond one week.

BRIGHT AND EARLY

_____
_____
_____
_____
_____
_____

MIDDAY

_____
_____
_____
_____
_____
_____

SLEEPY TIME

_____
_____
_____
_____
_____
_____

~DAY 2~

BRIGHT AND EARLY

_____
_____
_____
_____
_____
_____
_____

MIDDAY

_____
_____
_____
_____
_____
_____
_____

SLEEPY TIME

_____
_____
_____
_____
_____
_____
_____

~DAY 3~

BRIGHT AND EARLY

_____
_____
_____
_____
_____
_____
_____

MIDDAY

_____
_____
_____
_____
_____
_____
_____

SLEEPY TIME

_____
_____
_____
_____
_____
_____
_____

~DAY 4~

BRIGHT AND EARLY

_____
_____
_____
_____
_____
_____
_____

MIDDAY

_____
_____
_____
_____
_____
_____
_____

SLEEPY TIME

_____
_____
_____
_____
_____
_____
_____

~DAY 5~

BRIGHT AND EARLY

_____
_____
_____
_____
_____
_____
_____

MIDDAY

_____
_____
_____
_____
_____
_____
_____

SLEEPY TIME

_____
_____
_____
_____
_____
_____
_____

~DAY 6~

BRIGHT AND EARLY

_____
_____
_____
_____
_____
_____
_____

MIDDAY

_____
_____
_____
_____
_____
_____
_____

SLEEPY TIME

_____
_____
_____
_____
_____
_____
_____

~DAY 7~

BRIGHT AND EARLY

_____
_____
_____
_____
_____
_____
_____

MIDDAY

_____
_____
_____
_____
_____
_____
_____

SLEEPY TIME

_____
_____
_____
_____
_____
_____
_____

NOTES

www.ingramcontent.com/pod-product-compliance
Lightning Source LLC
Chambersburg PA
CBHW050504110426
42742CB00018B/3366